A souvenir guide

Hatfield Forest

Essex

National Trust

Welcome to Hatfield Forest

Hatfield Forest is the best surviving example in Britain of an almost complete royal hunting forest in working order. It has seen many owners, from kings to commoners.

Hatfield Forest is a managed landscape, which has been created through human intervention. The traditional woodland management techniques of coppicing, grazing and pollarding have been practised here for centuries.

The ecology and landscape of Hatfield Forest have been largely preserved thanks to centuries of traditional woodland and pasture management, and grazing by deer and cattle. There are now about 360 hectares (900 acres) of high-quality habitat for wildlife; it is home to over 3,500 species, many of which are rare and threatened. The hundreds of ancient trees provide the perfect habitat for some of the Forest's rarest insects, lichens and fungi.

'Hatfield is the only place where one can step back into the Middle Ages to see, with only a small effort of the imagination, what a Forest looked like in use.'

Oliver Rackham, *The Last Forest*

All in a name

The name Hatfield comes from the Anglo-Saxon *hoep feld*. *Hoep* means heath, an area of heather or similar vegetation, while *feld* is not a field as we know it, but an open space in sight of woodland.

Above Pollarded hornbeam on Bush End Plain

Left Fallow deer

Opposite Old and gnarled tree trunk in the Forest

An ancient landscape

Hatfield Forest has a history that goes back over 10,000 years, to the time of the Wildwood, when trees covered most of northern Europe.

Early inhabitants

Humans have lived in this area since at least Mesolithic times (10,000–4,500BC). The Forest would have supplied everything the settlers needed to be self-sufficient: timber for building and heating, and plants and animals for food and clothing.

Working with wood

Wood was of course an essential resource for these early peoples. During the Iron Age (800BC–AD43), man maximised the yield of timber from a single tree by coppicing it. But in areas where animals grazed, this technique was not very effective, as the new tree growth was soon nibbled away, often causing the tree's premature death. In order to avoid this problem, pollarding was developed.

Below View across the site of the Iron Age Fort at Portingbury Hills in the Forest

Above This is how the fort at Portingbury Hills may have looked during the Iron Age

Right These two drawings show the differences between coppicing (top) and pollarding (bottom)

Cut and come again

Coppicing is a woodland management technique which involves the repeated cutting and harvesting of small-diameter trees at or near ground level. Traditionally undertaken on an 18-year cycle, it now takes place every 35 years at Hatfield Forest. This results in a larger area being in the cycle at any one time.

Pollarding is another way of harvesting a tree for timber. Unlike coppicing, it is undertaken in open wood pasture. The practice involves repeatedly cutting a tree every 20 years or so at a height of 2 or 3 metres, so that new growth remains out of reach of the tallest grazing animal. Some pollards can live for over a thousand years, if kept in their pollarding cycle. There are 884 veteran pollards recorded at Hatfield Forest, making it of international ecological importance.

The Warren

An historically significant element of the Forest is its 17th-century rabbit warren.

Protecting the rabbits

The Warrener, whose job was to protect highly prized rabbits from robbers, lived in Warren House, a lodge just next to the Warren. This unusually designed house, built in the late 1680s, was made of handmade red bricks, rather than a timber frame as was more common at the time. Gangs of poachers could turn violent, which may explain why the house was built of such strong materials and also featured a look-out tower. *(Warren Cottage is a private residence, not open to the public.)*

Fighting back

If you visit the site of the Warren today, you will see it has a number of dead horse chestnuts above it. These trees were planted in the 1700s and have recently succumbed to Phytophthora and bleeding canker, two virulent diseases in horse chestnuts. The trees have been 'monolithed' by Forest staff, so that only the trunk remains. This stabilises the dead wood and keeps the tree standing for longer. Standing dead wood rots more slowly than wood on the ground, and so remains a habitat for longer.
The future of this area is uncertain. It could be returned to its Iron Age or medieval past, or be replanted to recreate a Georgian landscape (see pages 16–17). This is one of many long-term decisions which form part of the Forest's management plan.

Did you know?
Rabbits were introduced into Britain from the Mediterranean during the Middle Ages. Warrens were built underground or in 'Pillow Mounds', as the rabbits were not adapted to the cold British climate. The Warren at Hatfield Forest was built within the remains of an Iron Age settlement in Collins Coppice.

Opposite This Edwardian print shows a woodland scene with rabbits around their warren

Left National Trust Ranger cutting down trees in the Warren

Royal hunting ground

King Henry I declared Hatfield Forest a royal hunting forest in around 1100. He introduced fallow deer to England from Europe and protected them with strict Forest laws.

Poachers beware!

Fallow deer were prized royal possessions. Although Hatfield Forest was rarely hunted by the king, the fines imposed on poachers brought him income. Poachers were also punished with hanging, blinding and imprisonment. Other sanctions included being sewn into a deerskin and hunted down by dogs, or having your testicles cut off.

Rare survival

Forest Lodge is the only Medieval forest lodge in England the remains of which can still be seen above ground. Although a house still stands on the site, it has been much altered since its original building in 1510–20. Its location is significant: from here, much of the Forest can be seen, which suggests that this was the head keeper's residence. *(Forest Lodge is a private residence and is not open to the public.)*

The Doodle Oak

In about AD950, an oak sapling began to grow in the Forest, which was to become one of the two stoutest oak trees ever recorded in England (its circumference measured 18.2m). Known as the Doodle Oak, it last grew leaves in 1858, making it 908 years old when it died. The origin of its name is the source of many stories. It may be related to the word 'dool' meaning boundary. Another suggestion is that it may have been the 'oak of doom'. Yet another hypothesis is that the tree, featuring a very large base, may have been named because it was shaped like a 'doodlesack', the sack of a bagpipe.

Right Hunting Scene, from the Book of King Modus and Queen Ration, 14th century

Opposite This 15th-century illuminated manuscript shows hounds and mounted huntsmen chasing a stag through a forest. In the foreground, servants prepare to release more hounds

Ancient rides

Hatfield Forest has a fairly regimented design, with rides running through the woodland, separating areas of coppice and wood pasture.

This design dates back to the medieval period, when the rides (pathways) were created for the hunters on horseback. On either side would be a ditch and a woodbank construction. The woodbank would be topped with a hedge of dead sticks. This early form of fencing ensured recently cut coppice was protected from grazing animals. After about nine years, when the coppice trees were established, the dead hedge was removed and animals were allowed to graze freely.

Today you can walk along the medieval rides and see the remaining woodbanks. In the winter of 2011, a hectare (2.5 acres) of coppice was cut in Elgins Coppice. This area has been protected with a dead hedge made of brash (a by-product of the coppicing). In other parts of the Forest, baskets have been woven around individual coppice 'stools' to protect them from grazing.

Quirky coppices

The coppices have maintained their curious medieval names, including Hangman's, Spittlemore and Beggarshall. Many of them are named after local farms or the family who leased them at some time. Hangman's Coppice is not the site of an ancient gallows. Most likely, the coppice is named after a Mr Hangman.

Above Looking down an ancient ride through the coppice near Eight Wantz Ways in the Forest

Overleaf Fallow deer in a woodland clearing

Orchid haven

The ditches along the edges of the rides are systematically cleared to remove scrub plants such as bramble and tree saplings. Once the ditch is cleared, sunlight reaches the dormant wildflower seeds and they begin to flourish. The ditches are an excellent place to spot orchids, including the Pyramidal orchid, Early Marsh Orchid, Southern Marsh Orchid, Bee Orchid, Early Purple Orchid and Common Spotted Orchid.

Clockwise from top Common Spotted Orchid, Bee Orchid and Early Purple Orchid

Mixed fortunes

During the Middle Ages, the Forest changed hands many times. It was no longer owned solely by the king, but also by the gentry and commoners, who each had different rights.

Changing hands

In 1135 King Henry I (1068–1135) retained the rights to the land, but gave the Forest to Isabel, the daughter of the Earl of Chester, in exchange for part of her inheritance. Isabel had married into the Scottish Bruce family. From 1304–6, Hatfield Forest was owned by Robert the Bruce (1274–1329), who was King of Scotland. As King Edward I (1239–1307) also claimed to be King of Scotland, he confiscated Bruce's English estates, including Hatfield. Upon Edward I's death, Edward II inherited the Forest and passed it to his sister Elizabeth, wife of Humphrey VIII de Bohun.

The de Bohun family owned the Forest until it was inherited by Anne Stafford (1383–1438). She bequeathed it to her son, Humphrey, who became the 1st Duke of Buckingham (1402–60). He owned several large estates in England. After he was killed during the Wars of the Roses, his son Henry, 2nd Duke of Buckingham (1455–83), inherited the Forest but he was beheaded for committing high treason.

Above Edward II

Left Henry I

Above left Robert the Bruce and his second wife, Elizabeth de Burgh, from the Seton Armorial, 1591

Above right Sir Richard Rich, engraved by Francesco Bartolozzi in the 18th-century after a work by Hans Holbein the Younger

Hatfield Forest passed to Henry's son Edward (1478–1521). Initially he was a friend of Henry VIII (1491–1547), but his loyalty changed and, like his father, he was beheaded for committing high treason.

The next owner was the notorious Sir Richard Rich (1496–1567), who conspired against Sir Thomas More (1479–1535) and Bishop Fisher (1469–1535) and was influential in their execution. When he was promoted to the position of Lord Chancellor by Edward VI (1537–53), Sir Richard Rich was endowed with Hatfield Forest.

Meanwhile, the Barrington family claimed to have been the hereditary 'woodwards' of Hatfield Forest since before the Norman conquest. This meant they also had ownership rights.

Stalemate

In 1592 the Rich family split the ownership of the Forest between Lord Morley (1481–1556) and the hereditary woodwards, the Barringtons. There were also people with commoners' rights to graze their animals on the Forest. For the next 200 years, Hatfield Forest was not owned outright by any individual person. While one person may have owned the grazing rights, another owned the trees, and yet another owned land. These conflicting interests meant that no-one could really use another's share, so the Forest remained unchanged for hundreds of years.

It is these 500 years of indecision and changing ownership which have resulted in the survival of such an intact medieval Forest today.

The landscape transformed

From its 'creation' in 1100, Hatfield Forest remained virtually unaltered until the early 1700s when the arrival of the wealthy Houblon family brought significant changes.

The Houblons were a merchant family, who moved to England from France to escape religious persecution. Samuel Pepys made a number of references to them in his famous diary. Four of the five brothers were among the founders of the Bank of England and in 1694 Sir John Houblon IV (1632–1712) became its first Governor. His portrait was on the back of the £50 note until 2011.

'Five brothers *Houblon* … mighty fine gentlemen they are all.'

Samuel Pepys

Georgian alterations

In 1737, Jacob Houblon purchased the Hallingbury Estate, which included Hatfield Forest and the manor house, Hallingbury Place. The Houblons treated the Forest as an extension to their garden and were followers of the new Georgian trend for landscaped parks. They planted exotic trees, created an artificial lake and built a fashionable shell house for picnics. These alterations may have been influenced by Lancelot 'Capability' Brown, one of England's greatest landscape garden designers.

In the mid-18th century, Jacob Houblon's son made a very significant change to the Forest which is still visible today. The Shermore Brook was dammed, causing the marsh area to flood and a lake to be formed. Larger than it is today, the lake originally covered 3.2 hectares (8 acres).

Exotic imports

A symbol of wealth and status, exotic trees became the height of fashion during the Georgian period. Plant hunters travelled the world in search of new species to plant in British parks and gardens. Jacob Houblon was keen to experiment, planting specimens of the cedar of Lebanon, horse chestnut, giant redwood, Scots pine and Corsican pine around the artificial lake. At the same time, areas were cleared to create views.

Far left Sir John Houblon, first Governor of the Bank of England (1694–97) and Lord Mayor of London (1696)

Opposite The lake in November

Below Oak trees reflected in the decoy lake in autumn

The Shell House

Built in 1759, the Shell House was designed by Jacob Houblon's 17-year-old grand-daughter, Laetitia. Bright, exotic shells and coral were brought to England from the West Indies, possibly contained within the ballast from slave ships.

It was built to enjoy the new Georgian fashion for picnicking and was attached to a cottage, which was occupied by a housekeeper who kept poultry and peacocks. Above the door of the Shell House is a peacock, the breast of which is made from the fossil of an Inoceramus, a bi-valved mollusc from the Cretaceous period (145 to 65 million years ago).

The exterior of the Shell House is mostly decorated with flint and blue iridescent glass. The interior is resplendent with an ornate ceiling and fireplace decorated in shells and coral. The two pictures with shell-covered frames are thought to be original.

'Sir Jacob Houblon ... built a small House there for himself and friends to drink tea in and made a little Garden round it and cut several walks in the said coppice.'

Oliver Rackham, *The Last Forest*

Further changes

As well as making landscape (and architectural) changes to the Forest, the Houblons largely stopped pollarding the trees in the early 1800s when it became unfashionable. This cessation of a woodland management technique after centuries of use had significant ramifications for the future.

In order to be successful, coppicing and pollarding need to occur on a regular cycle. If not, the trees grow too large for the process to start again. Pollarded trees are characteristically squat with a fairly wide girth. The bolling (the place where the cut occurs at the top of the trunk) cannot support the weight of branches which have been left to grow too large. The branches form a huge sail, which when caught by the wind cause the tree to topple over or the branches to snap. Nowadays we mitigate this by tip-pruning the branches over a number of years. These old pollard trees cannot be harshly pruned as this would cause them too much shock and they might die. Instead, the tips of the branches in the upper canopy are pruned and the tree is gradually reduced in size.

Every veteran tree on the Forest has its own management plan. The aim is to keep veteran trees alive as long as possible, in order to preserve the important habitat they provide for birds, bats and invertebrates.

There is a gap in the ages of our pollards at Hatfield, so new maiden pollards are being created and we are undertaking the pioneering work of veteranisation (see page 23).

In 1857, the Houblon family invoked the Enclosures Act, giving them outright ownership of the Forest. Commoners were allocated land outside of the Forest's boundary. This process of 'buying out' the commoners cost the family over £3,000, approximately £130,000 today. The Houblons' reign ended in 1923, with the breaking up of their estate and demolishing of Hallingbury Place, which was sold for masonry.

Opposite left Shells and coral adorn the fireplace and mirror, creating decorative patterns

Opposite right Although simple in design, the Shell House brims with decorative detail, both inside and out

Below This painting suggests how the Shell House might have been used in the 18th century

Saved for the nation

Above Red Poll calf in the Forest

Opposite Buttercups in open pasture at Takeley Hill

Right Sale catalogue

Sir Edward North Buxton MP, a council member of the National Trust and passionate conservationist, had helped to save Epping Forest and the remains of Hainault Forest from destruction. In 1923, aged 83, he became greatly concerned about the plight of Hatfield Forest and decided to buy it for the National Trust at auction.

However, following an administrative error when his telegram went missing, Thomas Place purchased the Forest before Sir Edward. Place and a group of timber merchants ordered the felling of many trees, but the majority of the ancient trees were thankfully left intact.

Not to be defeated, Edward North Buxton negotiated the purchase of the Forest with Thomas Place. On his death bed on 1 January 1924, he concluded the first part of the sale. His sons Gerald and Anthony completed it and presented Hatfield Forest to the National Trust in 1924.

For ever, for everyone

In May 1924 Lord Ullswater, Vice President of the National Trust, opened Hatfield Forest to the public. A committee was formed, which included Teresa Buxton (Edward North Buxton's daughter) and local landowners. Hatfield Forest had been saved for future generations.

Long-term legacy

The traditional woodland management techniques of pollarding, coppicing and grazing continue today, but with modern tools. Some of the rides have been widened for improved access, but many still retain their medieval aspect. The layout of the rides and coppices and their names would still be recognisable to the people of the past.

Thanks to its continued management by past owners – and thanks also to their disputes and indecision – the Forest changed very little in its 900 years. The lack of ploughing has protected ancient earthworks such as Portingbury Hills and the Warren, and enabled yellow meadow ants (an ancient wood pasture indicator species) and Dog's Mercury (an ancient coppice indicator species) to flourish. In May and June the pastures are carpeted with 350 million yellow buttercup flowers. The continued grazing allows wildflowers to thrive and keeps the growth of scrubby trees, such as hawthorn, at bay. Today wood pasture is an internationally scarce habitat and to find it in such pristine condition makes Hatfield Forest extremely important.

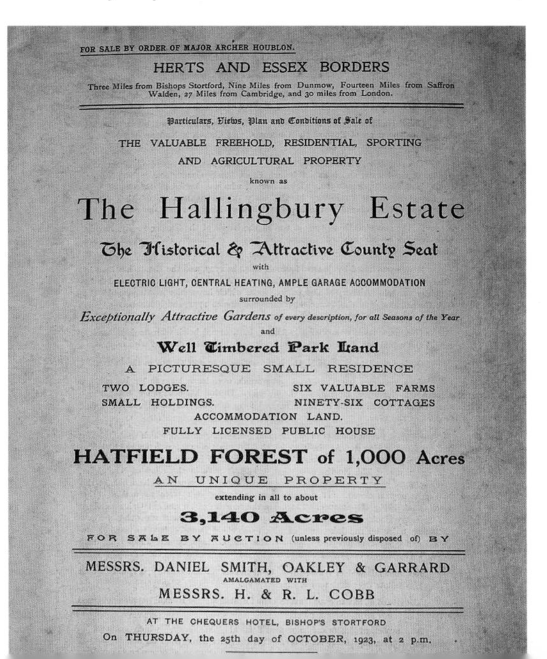

FOR SALE BY ORDER OF MAJOR ARCHER HOUBLON.

HERTS AND ESSEX BORDERS

Three Miles from Bishops Stortford, Nine Miles from Dunmow, Fourteen Miles from Saffron Walden, 27 Miles from Cambridge, and 30 miles from London.

Particulars, Views, Plan and Conditions of Sale of

THE VALUABLE FREEHOLD, RESIDENTIAL, SPORTING AND AGRICULTURAL PROPERTY

known as

The Hallingbury Estate

The Historical & Attractive County Seat

with

ELECTRIC LIGHT, CENTRAL HEATING, AMPLE GARAGE ACCOMMODATION

surrounded by

Exceptionally Attractive Gardens of every description, for all Seasons of the Year

and

Well Timbered Park Land

A PICTURESQUE SMALL RESIDENCE

TWO LODGES. SIX VALUABLE FARMS

SMALL HOLDINGS. NINETY-SIX COTTAGES

ACCOMMODATION LAND.

FULLY LICENSED PUBLIC HOUSE

HATFIELD FOREST of 1,000 Acres

AN UNIQUE PROPERTY

extending in all to about

3,140 Acres

FOR SALE BY AUCTION (unless previously disposed of) BY

MESSRS. DANIEL SMITH, OAKLEY & GARRARD

AMALGAMATED WITH

MESSRS. H. & R. L. COBB

AT THE CHEQUERS HOTEL, BISHOP'S STORTFORD

On THURSDAY, the 25th day of OCTOBER, 1923, at 2 p.m.

A haven for wildlife

Below The highly secretive water rail can be spotted in the Marsh, most often in winter when the vegetation has died down.

Opposite Blue tit on mistletoe

A National Nature Reserve (NNR) and Site of Special Scientific Interest (SSSI), Hatfield Forest is home to around 300 species of wildflower and 77 species of tree.

The Forest is an especially important place for fungi (650 species) and beetles (780 species), many of which are now uncommon across Britain.

The Marsh

The Marsh is the one of the most wildlife-rich areas of the Forest, with many rare species including the water rail. In 2010, it was restored to its former glory, opening up an historic view across the lake which had not been seen for over 100 years. The tall plants in its centre are reedmace, often mistakenly called bulrush. Up to 15 species of dragonfly and damselfly can be spotted in the summer months.

There's life in the dead wood

The Forest is not tidied up like a garden or park. Whenever possible, dead wood is just left in the location where it fell. This allows the wildlife present in the dead wood to move into the remainder of the tree or a neighbouring tree.

Underneath the mistletoe

Hatfield Forest contains one of the largest concentrations of mistletoe in the east of England. Mistletoe is partly parasitic as it steals water and nutrients from its host tree, which, at Hatfield, is field maple, hawthorn or lime. It is spread by birds, who rub the sticky fruit (and its seeds) into the bark of trees with their beaks. Wild mistletoe is a rare and protected plant, so please leave it to grow.

New techniques

Trees provide a home for a wide variety of species and these change over the lifetime of a tree. A dead tree which remains standing is a rare habitat. Some invertebrates can only live in standing dead wood. Once their host tree falls, they need to move to a nearby tree of a similar age. Due to the cessation of pollarding during the Houblons' ownership of Hatfield Forest, there is now a generation gap in the age of the trees.

Here at Hatfield, the Trust is pioneering a technique called veteranisation. Each year a few semi-mature trees are selected and prematurely aged by cutting off the larger limbs and by climbing the tree with spikes and boring into it with a large wood drill. These methods encourage fungal growth within the tree, which causes it to decay quicker than usual. The artificially aged trees then provide a habitat for a variety of wildlife which would otherwise die out.

Left The pond near Old Woman's Weaver in the northern section of the Forest

Key dates

Hatfield Forest looks virtually the same today as it did a thousand years ago. The oldest trees in the Forest have been growing throughout this time. Imagine what they have seen in their lifetime.

10,000BC
Wildwood covers most of the Northern Hemisphere

10,000–4500BC
Early settlers live in the woodland and use stone tools

AD410
The Anglo-Saxons name the forest *hoep feld*

1000
The oldest trees still standing begin to grow

1086
Hatfield Forest is mentioned in William the Conqueror's Domesday Book

1100
Henry I declares Hatfield a Royal Hunting Forest

1304
Robert the Bruce inherits Hatfield Forest

1306
Edward I, King of England, claims Hatfield Forest and it passes to his daughter, Elizabeth de Bohun

1446
Henry VI relinquishes all royal rights to the Forest and gives it to the 1st Duke of Buckingham

1521
Henry VIII confiscates the 3rd Duke of Buckingham's lands and holds onto Hatfield Forest until his death

1547
Edward VI gives Hatfield Forest to Sir Richard Rich

1737
Jacob Houblon buys Hatfield Forest

1923
Hatfield Forest is sold to Mr Place, a timber merchant

1924
Sir Edward North Buxton buys Hatfield Forest and donates it to the National Trust

2005
The Shell House is reopened after restoration